Praise for MODERNIZATION OF MUSIC

"MODERNIZATION OF MUSIC chronicles the most important achievement for the music industry in generations. Go behind the scenes with the players who were there and made it happen. E. Maxwell gets to the heart of the challenges we faced and how we overcame them to help songwriters for generations to come. This book is a great resource to those looking to see how progress is possible even in a partisan landscape and incredibly complex industry."

– DAVID ISRAELITE, PRESIDENT & CEO, NATIONAL MUSIC PUBLISHERS' ASSOCIATION (NMPA)

"Songwriting almost became an extinct profession in the modern age of digital music distribution because rules more than 100 years old governed how songwriter/composer compensation was set. However, the adoption of the Music Modernization Act changed those rules. E. Maxwell manages to boil this extremely complicated topic down in an interesting and understandable way. Every music lover can get a peek behind the curtain through MODERNIZATION OF MUSIC at how the rules were updated to give American songwriters a chance to earn a fair-market wage in the era of streaming music. Job very well done!"

– BART HERBISON, EXECUTIVE DIRECTOR, NASHVILLE SONGWRITERS ASSOCIATION INTERNATIONAL (NSAI)

MODERNIZATION OF MUSIC

First Edition
Released on Friday, November 13, 2020
ISBN: 9780578778044

Connect with E. Maxwell:
Website – www.emaxwell.online
Instagram – _emaxwell_
Facebook – MODERNIZATION OF MUSIC
by E. MAXWELL

Book designed by E. Maxwell
Cover Photo by Tom Murphy
Author Photos by Brendan Hayes

Printed in the United States of America

In memory of my grandfather, Jim Maxwell.
May your spirit live forever.

ACKNOWLEDGMENTS

Writing this book has been a great thrill. Thank you to Kris Ahrend, Senator Lamar Alexander, Larry Butler, Rick Giles, Ross Golan, Tyran Grillo, Senator Orrin G. Hatch, David Israelite, Tom Murphy, John Rich, and last but certainly not least, Bart Herbison, who helped guide me through the entirety of this project.

You all saw my vision and helped me bring it to light. For that, I am eternally grateful.

SETLIST

MODERNIZATION OF MUSIC

E. MAXWELL

IF THE LAST two years of my life were a river, then its headwaters would originate in the mountain of the music copyright industry. During that time, what initially began as a law school thesis took on a life of its own to become this short book. While writing my thesis, I quickly realized how complicated this area was and sought a better way to understand it, as law is for and by the people, not just those with some fancy degree.

Holding it all together has been my fascination with the Music Modernization Act, the passage of which signaled a watershed moment in music history—largely unnoticed amid the white noise of our current sociopolitical climate. The MMA, as it is often abbreviated, has offered no shortage of intrigue from conception to signing, and this book is an unprecedented overview of its history, significance, and implications for the future. While this book is intended as a reflection of time, the contents will hold true throughout the future.

My goal is to educate readers about the United States government's overregulation of the music industry, particularly with regard to songwriters. This book is intended to influence public opinion regarding how much songwriters should be paid. The U.S. government does not regulate how much a professional football player receives whenever they score a touchdown, so why should it limit how much songwriters get paid?

For too long, outdated laws prevented songwriters from receiving fair compensation in the digital age—a trend graciously bucked by the MMA. As the most important copyright overhaul to ever be enacted, the MMA begs for a lucid explanation in lay terms, which is precisely what you will find in the following pages. Although a complex subject on its own, this book reads much more like a story than a legal document. In addition to exploring the MMA itself, this book incorporates exclusive interviews with top music professionals and politicians across the U.S. to provide a nuanced, holistic picture of what recorded music is poised to become. They are the ones to make this a possibility—I am merely the messenger.

Personally, I work full-time during the day, study law at night, and have done nothing but eat, sleep, and breathe *MODERNIZATION OF MUSIC* over the past four months. Quite frankly, if it weren't for COVID-19, I might have never written it. But I'm a firm believer that life is what you make of it, and with the veil of distraction lifted, I couldn't very well pass up an opportunity to stoke the fires of my commitment to this project. That being said, this book is not about me—it's about our need for the songwriter and the importance of music to our society.

Songwriters are the farmers of the music industry. As such, their job is to cultivate a product that's then repackaged and brought to your (turn)table. But without the farmer, we would starve. And without the songwriter, our ears would wither like so much unirrigated corn. Music is, therefore, more than the soundtrack to our lives—it *is* our lives. Music, in its purest form, has no religion, color, political party, language barrier, or boundary lines. It teaches us about ourselves and one another. It is embedded in our individual and collective histories. And, it is a source of livelihood for many who can imagine doing nothing else. Music has always been my driving force, and I wouldn't be the person I am today without it. While I was never asked to write this book, I felt it was something I needed to do in return for the songwriter because of all the positive memories that music has given me.

Live concerts are where the human spirit *thrives.* People of different backgrounds, races, and places all come to sing and dance with friends they haven't met just yet. There is no competition in live music—only love. Music brings out the best in people, allowing us to see one another for who we truly are when our favorite song flows from the stage. And while we've barely exchanged a glance with the thousands swaying in unison around us, we share the same words, the same language, the same heartbeat.

There are some forces in life we cannot explain, and being at a show is one of them. The pandemic continues to rage as I write this and has made the magic of live performance feel like a dream of long ago. We're going through something unprecedented and must band together to stop this distressing force in its tracks.

In the face of all that is going on, we're also being hit with a mental health crisis like we've never seen before, as soberingly proven by rising suicide rates. If the world ever seems like it is crumbling around you, know that you're never alone. Seek help from available resources and those close to you, and always know that you are loved.

Take care of yourself.
Take care of each other.
Take care of our planet.
We will get by, and we will survive.

In the meantime, educate yourself about this extremely important piece of legislation, and you will be sure to gain a whole new appreciation for the songwriter and the music you already know and cherish, which continues to be a source of light in these dark times.

Flow,
E. Maxwell
Fall 2020

I

Setting the Stage

THE 21ST CENTURY is a paradox. On one hand, it redresses longstanding practices in technological clothing. On the other, it upholds new ideas by using materials that have been around for ages. Perhaps nowhere is this paradox so apparent as in the music industry. Living in the digital age, we produce and consume the largest amount of information that any generation on Earth has ever experienced. This has accustomed our brains to crave the gratification promised by such ubiquitous platforms as Instagram, Facebook, Twitter, YouTube, Spotify, Apple Music, and more. Consequently, our smartphones have become extensions of ourselves, constantly attuning our eyes and ears to what is happening in the parallel universe that is the internet.

If you're like me, you use your mobile device every day to keep up with our ever-changing world. Scientists have likened our use of social media to drug addiction. Whenever we get a "Like" on one of our Instagram posts, our brain releases dopamine. But here we find another paradox: we criticize social media for desensitizing us, all the while forgetting that human beings seek dopamine triggers in all sorts of activities. Should we, then, also lump those together with so-called addictions? Why should seeking confirmation or solidarity through an Instagram post, especially in these times of social distancing, be denigrated, when it may, in fact, bring people closer together?

My drug of choice is listening to music, and through its pleasures, I have access to an entire spectrum of emotional experiences that confirm what is most powerful and beautiful about the human condition. Music transcends, even as it may highlight, the social and political divisions in which we all seem to be drowning. Therefore, it is a binding force to which we all have a deeply personal connection and is nothing without the ears, hearts, and minds to absorb its implications.

With the simple touch of a finger—the most primal form of interaction one can imagine between flesh and an object—streaming services give us instant access to virtually any song we want. Thus, another new idea built around an action as ancient as humanity itself. While this has added a certain air of magic to the consumption of music, making it practically effortless for music lovers such as myself to access the high it provides, its impact has been far from positive across the proverbial board. Sadly, songwriters have been left behind due to outdated yet persistent laws in the United States.

For the past 111 years in the United States, laws have been in place that determine how much songwriters can be paid. For a nation that bases its claims to economic superiority on the tenets of capitalism, which on paper should reward individuals in direct accordance with their efforts, this is a slap in the face to everything such a system stands for. Why should songwriters be thrown to the wayside when their efforts are so vital to our social, political, and cultural identities? Somewhere along the way, common sense got left out of the equation.

To make matters worse, many pop singers today do not write their own music, and many behind-the-scenes talents, including composers, lyricists, and arrangers, are involved in the process. The paltry compensations already given to lone songwriters are further diluted when that process becomes collaborative.

Songwriters are the backbone of the music industry, regardless of who performs what they compose. Major music hubs in the U.S., such as Nashville, Los Angeles, New York City, and Miami, are filled with songwriters. Still, many have been struggling financially due to the antiquated laws governing their payouts and livelihoods. The regulations surrounding the music industry are massive and have been practically impossible to navigate without expert guidance. All of this, however, is changing with the Music Modernization Act. Adoption of the MMA will bring about a sea change in government regulation of songwriters' musical royalties befitting of the 21st century.

Before the MMA, the rates at which songwriters got paid were governed by a statute adopted by Congress in 1909 and two consent decrees in effect since 1941. The 1909 statute prescribed how mechanical royalty rates were set for songwriters. The consent decrees directed how "rate courts" would oversee the setting of performance royalties for two of the performing rights societies: the American Society of Composers, Authors and Publishers (ASCAP) and Broadcast Music Incorporated (BMI). Both were required to enter consent decrees administered by the U.S. Department of Justice's Anti-Trust Division to oversee rate-setting because they had no other competition. Over the years, other performing rights societies have emerged but are too small to be subject to such decrees.

While the MMA did not raise either ASCAP or BMI's performance royalty rates or the mechanical royalty rates for songwriters, the Music Modernization Act, more importantly, changed the way the two rates are set, which will now require judges to approximate what the free market will pay songwriters. The new "rate standard" is called the "willing buyer, willing seller" fair market value rate.

The Storytellers

IN PUTTING THIS book together, I couldn't very well neglect those whose creative endeavors have made the industry what it is today. In that regard, two names immediately came to mind: Rick Giles and Ross Golan. Knowing the depth of their contributions to our musical culture and wanting nothing more than to have their voices represented in this project, I was humbled and honored to sit down with each of them on separate occasions through the aid of technology. They graciously shared their thoughts on how music and politics have come to be increasingly, and unfortunately, intertwined and how the MMA will untangle some of the mess.

Rick Giles began his songwriting career in New York City in the 1970s before relocating to Nashville in 1983. Six months after his move, he scored a hit with Eddie Rabbitt's "You Put the Beat in My Heart."

In the nearly 30 years that followed, his songs were recorded by Reba McEntire, Rascal Flatts, Hall & Oates, Charley Pride, and more. His songs have spanned country, pop, rock, and R&B, netting him a total of 21 BMI and ASCAP awards. Most recently, his 1976 hit "Wham Bam" was featured on the soundtrack for Guardians of the Galaxy Vol. 2.

Here, Rick Giles shares his memories of the legislative seeds that would later blossom into the Music Modernization Act.

I retired almost eight years ago from Nashville. But I remember the bill was being worked on back then. Before, we always had a physical product, and even when we didn't get paid much, we could count on what we were going to be paid because there was a physical product. If you were on a million seller, you knew you would get paid a million times the statutory rate or whatever rate you had negotiated. So if it was going to be a million pennies, well, you knew it was going to be a million pennies. When I first started out in the music business back in the mid-70s, that's what it was: a penny a song. It was split, so if you had two cowriters and two copublishers, then everybody got a quarter of a penny.

Then the copyright law of 1976 was enacted, and it provided for an eventual raise. And in the heyday, in the '90s, we actually got to the point where we were splitting 9.1 cents.

Here's the thing: Nobody could have ever imagined what technology would be able to do, and when CDs came along, as long as nobody was able to make a CD, everything was fine. But once people could buy CDs you could record onto, they could make 100% perfect copies of the original product, and that was serious stuff. And when Napster came along, you could actually go online and find pretty much anything and download it if you had a fast-enough internet speed. Nobody had to buy a physical product after that.

I was not privy, or I didn't pay enough attention, to the people who were working on this legislation or their thinking around it, except that what they needed to do was to get companies like Spotify to finally say, okay, we owe you something and we agree to pay it to you. But with everything being computerized, everything being digital information, it is at least possible to get paid for every instance in which you're owed compensation. And that's a good thing. But it's inconceivable to me that, beginning in 2021, we're only now going to have all the proper copyright information associated with every song, when it has certainly been possible for years for all of this to come together.

99

Ross Golan is a multi-platinum-selling, multi-award-winning songwriter who has worked with top artists such as Justin Bieber, Ariana Grande, Snoop Dogg, Selena Gomez, Linkin Park, Maroon 5, and Keith

Urban, just to name a few. Golan is the producer of the podcast "And The Writer Is...," of which he also serves as host in Los Angeles. It has garnered over three million downloads to date.

Golan coauthored an initiative to include songwriters in the GRAMMY® Awards "Album of the Year" in 2016, and 2017 marked the first year a songwriter won. In 2019, he became the first songwriter to sit on the board of directors of the National Music Publishers' Association (NMPA) in its 103-year history. In 2019, Golan's concept album The Wrong Man *was released and opened as an Off-Broadway musical in New York City, directed by Hamilton's Tony Award-winning director Thomas Kail. While he has achieved much in his music career, among his most extraordinary feats is his leading role in organizing songwriters to help secure the passage of the Music Modernization Act. Here, Ross Golan shares his thoughts on the impact of the MMA on the music industry.*

I used to think having a degree in music would teach me how not to get screwed, but it ended up teaching me how I *was* getting screwed. For the last 150 years, nonunionized songwriters have yet to figure out how to control their own destiny. It's strangely archaic because of how many things that have happened since 1909 that matter in the world. We continue to be marginalized artists. I guess the assumption is that we should be happy to be here.

We have no middle class because there's no economics built around a middle class right now for songwriters, and there's barely a lower class to speak of. The music industry is continually looking the other way. And so, seeing that there was an opportunity for honest legislation, or potentially honest legislation, to move the ball forward, I couldn't wait to be a part of it.

To get the House and Senate to unanimously sign off on something, as they did when the MMA passed in 2018, is unbelievable. The one who did try to hold it up was Senator Wyden out of Oregon. We even put up a billboard in his hometown with the phrase "Why do you hate songwriters?" written on it. But there were also people like Senator Gardner out of Colorado who did a lot to get Sirius Radio on board.

It's hard to explain to songwriters that their livelihoods have been predetermined. Most of them still ask, "What can we do?" And I don't know what the answer is right now. We have an industry that was built around these archaic rules. So what do you do? Rebuild publishing? Rebuild master ownership? And who's going to fund that in the face of distributors and streaming services? It's impossible to really rebuild what has been refined to become a business within the confines of these 111-year-old laws. A lot of people have had issues with this part or that part of the MMA. My thought process is that we needed to start somewhere, like the Affordable Care Act did, in that it wasn't socialized medicine, but it at least got the ball rolling in creating a health care system for people who couldn't afford health care. Is the MMA the answer to everything? Clearly not.

Even sitting on the board for the NMPA, even having the education and experience within the music industry that I have, and even having the attorney and team that I have, I still have no idea why I get paid so little for the successful songs. There are people out there writing songs being cut by major artists on successful albums that might have 100 million streams on YouTube or Spotify and are unable to make a living wage off of them. I think we would all agree that 100 million streams is a great success. If you can't feed your family off of that, there's something wrong with the economics of our business. This is because I know that the value is so much more on the master side and the digital service providers' side. By not sharing the profits with those who created the music to begin with, you're essentially pricing them out.

The obligation of the music industry, and of other executives, is to help educate songwriters.

This is because there isn't a lot of information out there on how or why we get paid what we do because it fluctuates so quickly. It would take an attorney or someone with some sort of legal background to really know how they're getting paid as a songwriter. I have ten writers signed to me and my publishing company, and they're all younger than I am. *None of them understand how they're getting paid.* Very few people understand what a publishing deal actually is. So the odds of a songwriter being knowledgeable about their vocation is unrealistic.

But in the practical sense, as songwriters and as artists, *we sell air for a living.* Here in my studio, I'm surrounded by guitars, basses, and other instruments. These are the tools of my trade. My job is to create music and to entertain people, and I tell artists that all the time. Our job is to entertain the audience. When you look at people in a restaurant mouthing along to a song or people in an arena singing every word or clapping along, or you see people at a concert crying, or whatever it is, it's all because someone sat in their room and structured a piece of art to which you got emotionally connected and around which you then built your own memories.

In return, you have some people in streaming services assuming that the value of what we do is relatively worthless at this point because all they need is for artists to put up content and for fans of that artist to click on it. Quality isn't part of the equation. They make the same amount of money, regardless of whether the song is good. So I'm writing with the knowledge that people listen to music differently right now. A songwriter doesn't need to write their own song. A songwriter doesn't even need to write their artist's song. *A songwriter writes their artist's fans' song.* That's what really helps me become a more attuned collaborator.

I tell my writers that I'm not aiming for album cuts. I'm only aiming for hits. I'm only aiming for singles. If they fall into album cuts, I'll take that as a bonus because it keeps the ball rolling, and it's putting points on the board. But I don't want my writers aiming for album cuts anymore. I have album tracks with some of the biggest artists in the world that essentially generate *hundreds of dollars.* That's it.

Nothing good comes from a bunch of really cool-sounding songs, unfortunately. There's a big difference between good music and good songs. And I'm not in the business of making good music. I'm in the business of *making good songs.* I love good music. I will write good music for the right occasion. I will listen to good music often more than I listen to good songs because I find it less distracting and because it's not my business.

It has been exciting to galvanize our community to do something for each other in light of the MMA. This doesn't really affect me, but it does affect our community, and it affects my writers. We have come to realize that we can look out for each other. I started reaching out to my peers, who are writers and artists. I rarely ask them to do things, but when I asked them to do something to support their community, most were really excited to be a part of something bigger. And so, this has been a good catalyst for activism. It was nice to see something change. It has always been interesting to have conversations with songwriters about survival. That's what makes having a chance to modify the legislation so exciting. Maybe we are the generation to change all of this. It's because of this generation that we're actually likely to continue moving things forward.

I set up my podcast "And The Writer Is..." with the goal of documenting what it's like to be a professional songwriter. I once had a biography from A&E about the Brill Building on DVD, for example. I used to watch it all the time. Songwriters would tell these amazing stories about what it was like to be songwriters. But, you know, when you interview somebody who has a lot of accolades and a lot of success, they tend to only talk about the successes. However, I found myself getting more interested in how they survive in between the successes. What happens when they aren't successful? How do they make do when they need health insurance and have no union? How would we survive if SAG-AFTRA (Screen Actors Guild - American Federation of Television and Radio Artists) wasn't around? If you aren't a singer, you're kind of screwed unless you at least play an instrument, then maybe you can get health care through the union that way. What I love about the podcast is that we've been able to have real conversations about how to fail, not just how to succeed, as a songwriter.

I hope that there is a future where songwriters have the ability to create their own value, get health care, and be treated on an equal footing with the rest of the business. If terrestrial radio goes away, there's no American dream for songwriters. In digital radio, you're going to get one-sixth of that. And if you're going to be making money through streaming alone, I just don't know how songwriters are going to make a living. There's a reason why I'm trying to get all my writers to write as much as they can right now because I'm an optimist, but I'm pretty nervous about the future for songwriters.

Due to the MMA, we were able to make this conglomerate of trade organizations. We even got people to take precious time away from their work to call their U.S. senators. This proactiveness, was in many ways, *as big of a victory* as the bill itself. This was the beginning of uniting a community that really hadn't been united. All of this makes me hopeful about what's in store. Seeing a group of songwriters who've never taken any ownership of anything other than their successes—that would be real excitement. But if we can begin the conversation with a new generation, maybe then we can figure these things out.

"

The Collective

THE ORRIN G. Hatch–Bob Goodlatte Music Modernization Act, otherwise known as the Music Modernization Act, was signed into law on October 11, 2018 (H.R. 1551 Pub. L. 115-264) during the 115th U.S. Congress. The MMA is a combination of three bills previously introduced in Congress: the Songwriter Equity Act, the Compensating Legacy Artists for their Songs, Service, and Important Contributions to Society (CLASSICS) Act, and the Allocation for Music Producers (AMP) Act. It is the most significant piece of copyright legislation to ever come across the President's desk.

To best understand the complexities of the Music Modernization Act, one must first understand how artists and songwriters are paid.

First, there are two copyrights: one for the song, another for the record someone makes of the song—even if the songwriter and the artist are one and the same. The song copyright covers the composition, known in legalese as the "musical work" or "underlying work," to which literally different laws apply than to any recording of the work in question. The second is the "sound recording." Also known as the "master," this is a particular expression of the underlying composition, produced and recorded by the recording artist(s). In the simplest scenario—for example, the song "Everything's Right," as written and recorded by Phish—both copyrights, the song and their recorded version of the song, are both owned by the same legal entity. Yet this is not always the case. Whoever covers and records "Everything's Right" will only own the master recording copyright or their recorded version of the song. The composition rights will still belong to Phish.

Sticking to the songwriter copyright, many professional songwriters will engage a music publisher and sign an exclusive songwriter-publisher contract for an agreed term. Given that music publishing is built around the promotion and monetization of musical compositions, music publishers have a two-fold mission: to make sure that royalties are collected and paid to their songwriters and to search for further opportunities to have the songs recorded and performed live. Songwriters may also act as their own publishers.

Music publishing, as we know it in the modern age, began in the early 19th century, however much has changed since. In the past, publishers once earned money by putting compositions to paper—producing songbooks, distributing them to stores, and compensating authors for the commercial use of their works. This is one reason why music albums are called "records." They are literal documents of a creative act with both legal and temporal value.

Music publishers today generate revenues in a variety of ways, as in the newer model of streaming services, although their core role remains the same. Publishers have typically used third parties to collect both mechanical and performance royalties (stay tuned) for over a century yet maintain administrative responsibility and oversight.

There exist limited areas, such as lyric reprints and the use of songs accompanied by a visual medium (a.k.a. synchronization or "sync"), in which songwriter compositions fall outside of federal jurisdiction. In such cases, songwriters can negotiate in the free market and often receive up to 50% of the monies generated. The sound recording has also traditionally received a 50% share for use in film and television. This fact became a strong illustrative point for songwriters during the evolution of the MMA and previous legislative efforts to change the astonishingly lower royalty shares set by the Copyright Royalty Board (CRB) and ASCAP & BMI rate courts. The CRB for songwriters is comprised of a three-judge panel which oversees mechanical royalty proceedings for the musical work every five years. There is also the ASCAP and BMI rate courts, where separate federal judges formerly appointed for life determined performance royalty rates for songwriters. Songwriters argued that the rules governing both the CRB and rate courts should be changed to achieve rates more closely resembling those that negotiations in the free market would bring.

Under U.S. law, to use a songwriter's musical work copyright, the user must obtain both a mechanical license and a performance license.

To obtain a performance license, users, from bars to streaming companies to broadcasters, typically go to the songwriter's performing rights organization (PRO), be it ASCAP, BMI, Global Music Rights (GMR), or the Society of European Stage Authors and Composers (SESAC). American songwriters can belong to only one PRO at any given time, although they do have periodic windows in which they may switch to another. Their PRO issues a "blanket license" to users, who now have the right to all performances of that songwriter's compositions. When users, such as a streaming service, obtain performance licenses from the four largest American PROs, they are granted the blanket performance rights to almost every commercial composition. When users properly obtain a blanket license, they are not subject to copyright infringement claims on performance licensing. Neither must they worry about paying each individual songwriter. Instead, they pay the royalties due (subject to how they are using the music) directly to the PRO, which pays the songwriter. This system is much more efficient than the mechanical royalty system adopted by Congress in 1909.

The mechanical license is a "compulsory license" and, as such, gives songwriters or music publishers control only over who records a given song the first time. Once the first mechanical license is granted, anyone can record the song as long as they properly obtain a mechanical license. Lawful copyright protection is thus attached to original works of authorship fixed in any tangible medium of expression. When the copyright is obtained, the author of the musical work gets an exclusive right to reproduce and distribute the musical work, perform or display the musical work publicly, and create derivative works based on the musical work.

Before the adoption of the MMA, a music user had to individually obtain the mechanical licenses to songs—sometimes more than 100 million such licenses in the case of a streaming service. Over time, private companies such as the Harry Fox Agency (HFA) or Music Reports Incorporated (MRI) were established to secure such licenses. The process was long, complicated, and fraught with data errors. And if a streaming service delivered music that was improperly licensed, they were committing copyright infringement and became subject to fines as high as $150,000 per stream!

The MMA created the first-ever American entity that would issue blanket licenses for mechanical rights. That entity is called The Mechanical Licensing Collective (MLC) and is set to fully begin operations on January 1, 2021. It issues blanket licenses very similar to those issued by PROs for performance royalties. The MLC was designated to administer and license mechanical royalties for digital streams and downloads only. They do not compete with the PROs and, by statute, cannot oversee performance royalties.

To find out more about this state-of-the-art globally recognized data and technology startup being instituted in Nashville, I sat down with The MLC Chief Executive Officer Kris Ahrend via Zoom.

Kris Ahrend started his career in the music industry working for Sony Music, where he provided legal services to all of Sony's U.S. divisions. Before being named the first CEO of The MLC, Ahrend was the President of U.S. Shared Services and led the development and launch of Warner Music's Center of Excellence for Shared Service. Ahrend also serves on the boards of the Nashville Chamber of Commerce and the Nashville Downtown Partnership and is a member of the Music City Music Council. Ahrend has had a substantial legal career in the music industry, and he is the most qualified to help bring music licensing to greener pastures.

We're a new collective management organization (CMO). We'll be administering a newly created blanket mechanical license in the U.S. available to digital audio services that offer interactive streaming and downloads. Starting January 1, 2021, those services will have the ability to secure a blanket license that allows them to use any song in the world on their U.S. services. The MLC will then administer that new blanket license.

In connection with administering the new blanket license, The MLC will also establish and maintain a public database of musical works ownership data. The public part of that is *key*. There are lots of musical works databases right now, owned by private companies. The MLC's data must, by law, be publicly available both for individual searches and bulk downloads so that anyone can access the musical works ownership data we maintain.

Each digital audio service that secures the new blanket license will be required to provide The MLC with usage files reporting the number of times each sound recording was used on their service each month and the corresponding mechanical royalties for the musical works embodied in those sound recordings. Once The MLC receives those usage files, we will match the sound recording usage data with the musical works data we maintain in our database. This matching process will enable us to determine which music publishers, administrators, and self-administered songwriters are entitled to receive a portion of the mechanical royalties we collected from the digital services.

While the blanket license we will be administering will only be available to digital audio services that operate in the U.S., the mechanical royalties we collect could potentially be payable to companies and individuals anywhere in the world—so The MLC will wind up paying people around the world. Because the music industry has become so global, with the U.S. market being the largest market, you could have a songwriter based in Japan who writes a song that's performed by a Japanese artist. But that sound recording still winds up being available on Spotify in the U.S., in which case our job would be to make sure that the songwriter, or the publisher representing that songwriter or the CMO in Japan that they're affiliated with, receives their share of mechanicals for all streams of that song in the U.S. market.

Another great feature of The MLC is that we're governed exclusively by a board of stakeholders made up of three groups: self-administered songwriters, large music publishers, and smaller music publishers. There is a segment of our board that has to be comprised of publishers who meet a relatively small revenue or market share threshold and are not among the five largest publishers. That group of smaller publishers is guaranteed to have representatives on our Board.

We started to get things up and running at the beginning of 2019. When I joined, I was the first employee—we've since hired more than 40 additional employees. We've also launched a number of initiatives and done a lot of outreach over the spring and summer. We began rolling out the initial version of our new user portal at the end of September 2020, which will allow members to see their data. We refer to January 1, 2021, as the first official date of our full operations because that's when digital audio services will be able to begin operating under the new blanket license.

The user portal is a brand-new piece of technology. It's a clean, user-friendly interface that's designed for individuals. Whether you work at a big company or a small publishing company, or you are a self-administered songwriter, the portal is designed to provide you with the ability to see your data, make changes to that data, or submit new works registrations. The first version of the portal is live now. This version allows people to see their works data, submit new registrations, and edit those existing registrations. We will launch other features, like the royalty component, next year, when we begin receiving and processing royalties. After that, we will add additional features that help members clean up and analyze their data. We'll also be making lots of smaller improvements along the way.

There were a lot of reasons The MLC decided to locate its headquarters in Nashville. Nashville is a hub for music publishing and has been for decades—as a result, a large concentration of publishers and writers are based here. It made sense for us to be in Nashville for that reason because it will enable us to interact regularly with our Nashville-based members. Nashville is also a place where people in the industry frequently travel for business. If you're in the music publishing business based in L.A., New York, Miami, or any other city in the country, there's a good chance your business will bring you to Nashville at some point. When people come to Nashville for business, we'll be able to meet with them in person then, too. Nashville's central location is also beneficial, as it places us between the East Coast and West Coast time zones, which makes it possible for us to be available to members on both coasts during their local business hours. Increasingly, Nashville has become a hub for administrative operations within the music industry, so locating The MLC here aligns us with those administrative operations. Finally, Nashville offers a great standard of living for our employees.

Financially, there are many benefits The MLC will bring to songwriters and publishers. First is the centralized administration that The MLC will provide. This will be a huge benefit for songwriters and for publishers by making it easier for any of our members to maintain their ownership data because we'll now have that centralized database of musical works ownership—unlike before when they had to maintain that data in the databases of multiple private administrative companies and digital services. We'll also be able to deliver one royalty statement showing the blanket licensing activity from all the digital services. Second, we will be matching everything in the first instance, even if a service maintains a direct deal with a publisher. Doing all of the matchings on the ownership side is going to eliminate variances from service to service or administrator to administrator. In the past, different services sometimes made different matches because they were using different data. Third, centralized administration should allow The MLC to provide our members with greater transparency. By maintaining a public database, every publisher or songwriter will be able to check the accuracy of the data we are using to distribute royalties. If you're a writer who has written 50 works that have been commercially released, you can look very easily at your 50 works and see whether the data we have for those works is accurate. If you're a publishing company, you can focus on the data for the works that you manage. Our portal will allow everyone to see and improve the quality of their data more easily and effectively, which will lead to improved payments. Fourth, one interesting thing we secured in the regulatory process is the requirement that services provide links for our portal members to the audio on those services that correspond with the data we get. Thinking ahead to unclaimed and unmatched activity— the money that doesn't get connected because someone didn't claim it or because we don't have all the data—we will eventually be able to enable our members to listen to the sound recording that corresponds with unmatched activity, which should help them claim unmatched activity more easily. Interpreting data can be hard because it's often just a series of numbers or words—that's not the language of music. If you can listen to the sound recording represented by that data and recognize the musical work it features as your own, it'll be much easier for you to identify your work.

One last point about having better data— we launched our Data Quality Initiative earlier in the spring of 2020. That initiative essentially allows people to perform a comparison of the data they've got in their systems with our data. We then send them a discrepancy report that only shows where there are differences between the two sets of data. That's a great way for people to really hone in on what's different and then determine whether there is an error on their end or ours. If you're managing hundreds of thousands of works, being able to hone in on those discrepancies is really important because otherwise, they're like needles in a haystack. If the haystack is big enough, you never see the needles. Our report only shows you the needles. This, too, will ensure better payments.

The MLC is a non-profit governed by our stakeholders, the people we serve. Membership is free, and by law, digital services will be required to pay our operating costs fully. Unlike other collective management organizations, which fund operations by essentially taking an administrative fee—we can pass *100%* of what we receive to our stakeholders and members. I think that's a pretty extraordinary feature of the law. By being a membership organization, we have a much greater ability to partner with our members to ensure we are serving them well. We also hope they will help us serve them by playing their part and helping us maintain the quality of their musical works data. The MLC's transparency is also about *empowerment*. It's about putting creators and publishers in a position where they can more clearly see how the system works in order to make sure it's working effectively for them.

When there are these sea changes in the music industry, the initial challenge is just helping people understand what's changing and what will impact them directly. It's therefore really important for anyone who works on the songwriting side of the business to do as much as they can to learn about what we're doing, how it's going to change, and how it can impact them. The other side of the coin is that change is hard and simply takes time. So, for us, The MLC is not just a moment in time. We won't be able to just flip a switch and change everything overnight. Progress will take time, so we need to create a culture of continuous improvement that always encourages our team to strive to make things better.

It's going to take a few years for the data to get better, for people to get used to engaging with the data in a different way, and to take advantage of the tools that we're putting out there. License availability for us is the start of a race and a partnership with our members that never ends. I want to encourage our members to moderate their expectations. Over time, incrementally, we're going to make things better, and in very significant ways. I hope that people will stay with us, remain engaged with us, and recognize that we can only do this together. Change takes time, *but change is worth it*. We're excited to help lead that change!

"

A Minor Miracle

CONTINUING ON WITH the nuts and bolts, there are three key types of publishing royalties/income that adhere to the three subsets of composition copyrights: mechanical royalties, public performance royalties, and synchronization license fees.

Mechanical royalties originally were so named because the 1909 statute establishing how they would be set was tied to the price of sheet music and mechanical player piano rolls. Today, mechanical royalties compensate songwriters for the reproduction of their compositions via payment by those who record and distribute the musical work on either a physical medium, such as a compact disc or vinyl, or place the song on a subscription music service.

There are different kinds of streaming music offerings in today's market. When a consumer subscribes to an "interactive" streaming model, that means they literally interact with their song choices by "choosing" or "controlling" their playlist on a subscription music service. Interactive streaming generates both a mechanical royalty for songwriters and a performance royalty. In the case of "non-interactive" streaming services, such as Pandora was when it was launched, customers have very limited control over what they hear, as these services function more like (or may actually be) streaming radio stations. Only performance royalties are paid to songwriters when the service is non-interactive.

In the past, mechanical royalties were traditionally higher than performance royalties based on consumers' ability to hear a song whenever and as many times as they wanted. Mechanical royalties were paid for physical products such as records, tapes, and CDs. No performance royalty was collected on a physical product. Because interactive streaming has elements of a physical product in the sense of being able to control the customer's playlist and is also "performed" through a digital medium, songwriters receive both a performance and a mechanical royalty for interactive streaming activity.

On-demand downloads and physical sales are different, as the mechanicals go to the owner of the sound recording first. In the commercial music industry, said owner is typically a record label having to distribute the royalties due to the publisher. Mechanical royalty rates have been set by the CRB, depending upon whether the song is recorded on a physical or digital medium. Mechanical royalties for digital downloads and physical mediums are currently set at a flat rate of 9.1 cents per copy for songs less than five minutes and 1.75 cents per minute for songs longer than five minutes.

Public performance royalties compensate the songwriters and their music publishers for the performance or display of their musical works. Every time a composition is publicly performed—in the form of a digital stream, radio broadcast, office playlist, on TV, in live performance venues, etc.—the rights owners get paid. Public performance royalties for songwriters are managed, collected, and distributed by performing rights societies or PROs. Recording artists receive a separate, and if they are also the songwriter, additional public performance royalty for the use of the sound recording from digital streaming alone and not from traditional radio or television broadcasting, nor from performances at live venues. This royalty stream is licensed and collected directly by the record label or by SoundExchange, a nonprofit entity set up by Congress to handle all public performance royalties relevant to digital music.

To legally perform music in a public setting, broadcasters obtain blanket licenses on songs they play, typcially securing the blanket licenses from PROs. This means that whenever music is played in public, there is most likely a blanket license behind it. PROs offer licenses with more restrictions, but the blanket license concept has been useful in allowing broadcasters and streaming services to secure licenses that cover most of the commercial repertoire of music.

Synchronization license fees, unlike mechanical and performance royalties set by government-created entities, are negotiated in the free market. Every time a musical work is used as a part of any other type of content that includes video, such as a movie or television/streaming program, permission must have been granted from the copyright owners. Sync agreements must be negotiated by both composition and sound recording owners, meaning that the licensors have had to go through both songwriters' and recording artists' representatives. Synchronization royalties have historically been shared equally between the publishing and recording arms of the music business.

Most successful songwriters share a 75/25 percentage split with their publishers. Artist and record label deals are all negotiated separately, and most don't get anywhere close to a 50/50 split. Artist deals, also called 360 deals, include shares of tour, merchandise, and other revenues.

To best describe how songwriters have had to jump through great hoops to receive royalties determined by the government, I sat down via Zoom with none other than David Israelite, the mastermind and architect of the MMA, to help pull back the curtain even further.

David M. Israelite is President and CEO of the National Music Publishers' Association (NMPA), a position he has held since February 2005. Israelite is responsible for overseeing all aspects of the NMPA's operations located in Washington, D.C., from legal strategy and implementation to government affairs and advocacy. His tenure to date has produced landmark successes on behalf of publishers, including the Music Modernization Act and the largest Copyright Royalty Board rate increase in history, in addition to groundbreaking industry collaboration in royalty rate agreements and raising the profile of the publishing community. He has been named among

Billboard's Power 100 multiple times and currently serves on several boards, including the Songwriters Hall of Fame and Special Olympics DC.

Most people don't understand that songwriters—and the revenues they make—are heavily regulated by the government. Either because of a law that was passed in 1909 or a consent decree that was imposed in 1941. In 1909, Congress thought that the music publishing industry had a monopoly on player piano rolls. These were actual physical things that you would stick into a player piano, and the piano would play a song without anyone manually operating the piano. It was the precursor to sticking a physical piece of music—a vinyl record, cassette, or a CD—into a player and playing a song. Back then, this was all done on a piano.

Congress thought that music publishers had too much market concentration, thus they passed a law that said music publishers representing songwriters had to license their copyright for player piano rolls. They could not deny a license. The government set the price at one cent, and ultimately, *some seven decades later*, Congress finally realized they had to adjust that number based on what was going on in the marketplace. But they never seriously considered getting rid of it.

All through the era when record labels made records and sold them, the same law applied. Then, when we got to digital and companies instead sold downloads, the same law applied. The system really broke down when interactive streaming companies entered the picture with a different equation altogether. Now, if you were a record label that sold a physical good to a consumer like a vinyl record or CD, you would go and license the songs on that record from the publishers, collect the money, and pay them. You knew who wrote these songs because the artist who recorded the songs was the record label's artist. It was a very small, contained, controlled project to put out an album.

What Apple, as the dominant player in downloads, said to record labels is *we don't know who wrote these songs.* So you record labels keep paying those songwriters, we'll just give you all the money while you pass the money on to the songwriters who are owed on this particular song that we've sold as a download.

This is because there are two different copyrights—one from the songwriter for the song and one from the artist for the recording of the song. When streamers got into the business, the record labels stopped passing through the publishing rights. They basically said to the streaming companies— it's not our responsibility you do it.

The streaming companies who would open

up their platforms with 40 million songs had no idea who owned the actual copyrights of the songs. So they would go out into the marketplace, hire vendors, and ask them to do their job for them, which *would determine* who they were supposed to pay on the songwriter side. If the vendor made a mistake or the vendors didn't know the answer, then the streaming company became a copyright infringer and was liable to lawsuits. That's why the system broke away from this 1909 law. Despite being unfair to songwriters, the law worked at least until the point we got to streaming companies around the year 2000.

Fast-forward to today, and songwriters are probably the most heavily regulated small businesspeople in the country. The obvious question is: If they're regulated due to these antiquated standards prescribed from 1909 and 1941, isn't it time they got out of that regulation? The simple answer is that we would love to get out of the regulation, but politically, we've been unable to do that because there are so many people that benefit from us being regulated in this way. Everybody who pays for music likes the system the way it is because we can't say no. And so, songs are generally being undervalued in terms of meaning and how they're used.

So here we are, stuck in this system of having prices set. We would love to get out of it. We'll keep fighting to get out of it. But it would take an act of Congress to change that. When you're fighting against combinations of broadcasters and giant digital companies and bars and restaurants and hotels, all of whom are unified in wanting music regulated—it's politically near *impossible*. A separate issue is that if you're going to be regulated and the price is set by the government, does the process itself work or not?

What we found over time is that the process was broken. So we had a choice. The choice was, do we continue to live under a regulated system where the process doesn't work, or do we try to fix the process to work, even though we would rather not be in the process, to begin with? It became very apparent that because the process was broken, the people who use the music, mostly the digital technology companies now dominating the delivery of music to consumers, were willing to give things of great value and agree to get the system fixed.

The entire premise of the MMA was a bargain between songwriters and digital companies. Everything else that's in the MMA was like a train car that was attached to someone else's locomotive—they got pulled across the finish line. The reason why the MMA was passed into law is because of this basic trade. The trade was this— for digital companies that use songs—we would create a new system for them to license those songs under this unfair compulsory license that we couldn't get out of. We would make it work for them, so that they weren't exposed to litigation by doing it improperly. In exchange for fixing it, they would give us a list of things that we cared about. That list is contained within the MMA.

The streaming companies are going to pay for everything, which means songwriters will no longer have a commission taken off the top. They're going to fund a database to be created, which will be of great value to everybody. They're going to give us an audit that we didn't previously have and actually pay for us to audit them because they're covering all the costs. Lastly, we changed the rules of the trials that set prices in a way that favors songwriters.

It is amazing that we got all of the relevant parties to agree on what to do throughout this process. There were really four clusters of constituencies that had to agree. You had the first cluster, made up of the songwriters, publishers, PROs, and other interested parties. You had the artists, record labels, and music unions as a second cluster. You had the digital companies, which have different focuses, as the third. And then you had the broadcasters, who are always involved in legislation like this. We had to get all four of them to get on the same page. *It was a minor miracle.*

99

Hatching a Plan

IN THE DIGITAL delivery era of music, it has become increasingly difficult for songwriters to sustain careers, and many have had to leave the profession. Before digital, most successful professional songwriters who wrote for the commercial music market made a living from album cuts and the occasional single release. There were more bona fide record labels, and more artists signed to labels. Songs were released more frequently and stayed on charts for much shorter periods of time, resulting in a far greater number of opportunities for songwriters to receive royalty income.

During such times, there was much less economic pressure from record labels to sign artists who also wrote their own songs. All of this translated into a larger number of spots available at music publishing companies for songwriters, particularly those not also pursuing record deals and careers as artists in their own right.

The Nashville Songwriters Association International (NSAI) has guesstimated that up to 90% of viable publishing deals available to professional songwriters in Nashville were lost. There may have been other spots for songwriters who had songs that still generated income, but spots for those whose deals depended on generating current activity and getting new cuts dwindled. Songwriters were earning so little per stream that a song with two cowriters, each of whom had a music publisher, generated less than $200 for each songwriter per 35 million streams! More and more songwriters found themselves out of work as the industry adjusted to digital streaming.

Bart Herbison, Executive Director of the Nashville Songwriters Association International, had much to say regarding the passage of the MMA, as he served one of the most vital roles in its institution. The NSAI is the world's largest not-for-profit songwriters' trade association and therefore has a vested stake in the outcomes of any new legislation related to the music industry. Established in 1967, the NSAI's membership of nearly 5,000 spans the United States and many other countries.

Under Herbison's leadership, the NSAI gained prominence in the national legislative arena. Below, you will find a statement from Herbison, with more to follow in the upcoming pages.

The 1909 Copyright Act language that governed the process of setting mechanical royalties through the CRB, as well as the World War II-era ASCAP and BMI consent decree rules that governed the process of setting performance royalties, were so outdated that the disparity in the income generated between the musical work (song) and the sound recording (record) copyrights grew as high as 1700%! The record copyright was earning as much as 17 times the song copyright, and this forced many songwriters to leave the business due to a lack of opportunity to earn a sustainable income.

99

The federal government regulates about 75% of what songwriters are paid. In other words, all song-generated income (excepting synchronization) is regulated. The Music Modernization Act did not change writer royalty rates; rather, it changed the rules by which both mechanical and performance royalties are set. The MMA now requires CRB judges and ASCAP and BMI rate court judges to look at what the market would pay songwriters. Previously, those judges could not consider deals such as those negotiated in the free market by record labels when they considered rates. Now, such consideration is required. Moreover, whereas ASCAP and BMI's court judges were previously appointed for life, they will now be selected at random for rate proceedings.

While writing this book, there was someone who I felt was absolutely crucial to include.

I am, of course, referring to the man who stood behind this legislation before its inception. Needing no introduction, the bill's namesake: Senator Orrin G. Hatch from Utah. Senator Hatch was kind enough to provide me with the following statement concerning this landmark piece of legislation.

The heart of the bill is the creation of a mechanical licensing collective to administer reproduction and distribution rights for digital music. One of the driving forces in recent years of the decline in songwriter royalties has been the transition to digital music. This may seem a bit surprising, as one might think that the availability of millions of songs at the click of a mouse would lead to more royalties, given that more music than ever before is now available instantaneously.

But the problem is that these big digital music companies, like Pandora and Spotify, with their catalogs of millions of songs, simply don't have the capability to find every single songwriter for every single one of their songs. Tracking down the recording artist—that is, the singer—usually can be done. But finding songwriters is a different story.

And so the bill creates a mechanical licensing collective that is tasked with identifying songwriters, matching them to sound recordings, and then ensuring that the songwriter actually gets paid. Importantly, this collective will be run by songwriters themselves and by their representatives in the publishing community.

This is an enormous victory for songwriters. For the first time in history, songwriters and their representatives will be in charge of making sure they get paid when their songs get played. The bill also changes the rate standard for reproduction and distribution rights to ensure that songwriters get paid a fair market rate. And it provides important protections to digital music companies. It creates a blanket digital license for companies like Pandora and Spotify so that they can have certainty that they won't be sued when they offer songs for download or interactive streaming. It also provides a liability shield against past infringement provided certain conditions are met, again so that digital music companies can have certainty going forward.

The Music Modernization Act also makes important changes to performance rights. It creates a federal performance right for pre-1972 sound recordings and moves our licensing laws away from the patchwork of inconsistent state laws and toward a more uniform, coherent federal standard. It ends the rate carve-out that legacy cable and satellite providers have enjoyed for two decades that has allowed them to pay below-market rates and stave off meaningful competition. This will result in fairer rates for recording artists and create a more level playing field for new market entrants.

The legislation also provides that rate proceedings for performance rights will rotate among judges and that judges may consider sound recording royalty rates when setting corresponding rates for musical works. And it makes a clear statement that the Department of Justice should work with Congress to ensure there is a proper framework in place to administer performance rights for musical works in the event the Department decides it's time to sunset the ASCAP and BMI consent decrees.

Lastly, the bill puts in place a formal process for producers, sound engineers, and other behind-the-scenes players to receive a share of performance royalties. This will help ensure that all of the participants in the music-making process are fairly compensated for their contributions.

The Orrin G. Hatch–Bob Goodlatte Music Modernization Act is a comprehensive piece of legislation that will have wide-ranging impacts across the music landscape. It touches all sectors of the music industry and makes important reforms to ensure that songwriters, musicians, and other key contributors to American music are treated fairly.

There's a reason this bill passed the Senate unanimously and shortly thereafter became law—all sides of the music industry came together to find a way to make our music laws better. To make them function properly. To update them for the digital age. No side got everything it wanted. But everyone got something. And at the end of the day, we have a piece of legislation we can all be proud of. **"**

What Unites U.S.

O N DECEMBER 11, 2018, President Donald Trump signed the MMA into law, witnessed by a collective group of music industry executives and recording artists such as Kid Rock, Beach Boys singer Mike Love, soul singer Sam Moore, and John Rich. Changes under the MMA should reward higher rates for songwriters and publishers.

Reactions to the passage of the MMA have been extremely positive. These reactions can be seen across the board, spanning from the President of the United States to music industry executives and songwriters alike. "The Music Modernization Act closes loopholes in our digital royalties' laws to ensure that songwriters, artists, and producers receive fair payment for licensing of music," Trump said just before signing the law. "They were treated very unfairly. They're not going to be treated unfairly anymore."

Likewise, Senator Lamar Alexander, a true champion of the MMA, has heralded its passage. Senator Alexander has tremendously represented the interests of all musicians throughout his many years of dedicated public service to the great state of Tennessee.

When I was governor of Tennessee, I tried to think of what united our long, skinny state—from Memphis to Mountain City—and the answer was always music. But for far too long, too many of our songwriters have been struggling to earn a fair-market value for their work. To give you an idea of what this really means for songwriters, a few years ago, I chatted with an older couple outside a pharmacy and I said, "How're y'all doing?" and the lady said, "We're just falling apart together."

A few days later, I was with songwriters Lee Brice, Billy Montana, and Jon Stone and told them the story. They said, "I think we could do something with that." And they wrote a song called "Falling Apart Together" and gave me ¼ of the song for suggesting the title because that's the way Nashville works.

Lee Brice put it on one of his albums, and I was paid ¼ of the royalties each time the song was played. Lee Brice is a pretty well-known singer, so you might think that would add up to a lot of money, but in 2016 my royalties only added up to $101.75. If you are a songwriter living in Nashville, you can't make a living on that.

This legislation, crafted working with songwriters, music publishers, and digital music companies is a huge step forward for what is the lifeblood of the music industry: songwriters. I was proud to work in the Senate to help pass this bill and give our nation's songwriters the fair pay they have earned.

To hear the first-hand account of the bill's historic signing at the White House and to gain an artist's perspective on the MMA, I was able to sit down via Zoom with country music superstar John Rich of Big & Rich. John has served as a substantial advocate for songwriters, and his experiences both within and looking at the music industry from the outside provide valuable insight into the subject at hand.

America invented rock and roll. America invented country music. The whole world has chased us. It continues to chase us, and probably always will because America gives us the right to pursue happiness. It's the American dream. It doesn't put any structures around us to slow us down. With that comes freedom of thought, freedom of expression, freedom of speech, and every other freedom we have. As it says in the Declaration of Independence, we are endowed by our creator with certain unalienable rights. We wake up every morning in this country with our minds on fire because we know we're allowed to have our minds on fire. And we have a system that nourishes those ideas to come to fruition. That's why America leads the world in music and creativity. Those were the kinds of thoughts going on in my mind as I stood there in the Oval Office, watching the President's ink pen hit the page.

We had to get everyone in Washington, D.C., conservative and liberal alike, in one room and make them listen to us. To be there in the White House with President Trump when he signed it, it was a huge honor. As the only cowboy hat in the room, I knew I was representing thousands and thousands of country songs—past, present, and future. It wasn't something I took lightly.

As I watched the President sign it into law, I thought about how this stepped *outside* the realm of politics. Because people, especially artists, who hate this President and his politics benefitted tremendously from him signing that piece of paper. The same would have been true had it been a Democrat signing it against the outcry of conservative artists. To me, it was quite an exclamation point on the *power and importance of music.*

I was grateful to have been asked to be there. I have advocated for many things in our industry, knowing they're going to help a lot of people who don't see eye to eye with me. But again, being a songwriter isn't a political thing. It's actually a very rare thing to be, especially a good one or someone who dedicates their entire life to it.

A record label worth billions of dollars can't buy what's inside of the songwriter's head. They can throw all the money they have at the wall, but it won't just appear. In the end, the slickest, most well-endowed institutions will always come to the guy with the old banged-up guitar, his pencil, and a piece of paper. "We need three big hit songs," they say. "Have at it." And they wait, utterly dependent on what he produces.

The Music Modernization Act forces us to recognize the fact that somebody has to create the music we love and that it's priceless. All told, the Music Modernization Act is a good start, but I do think there are more things that need to be added to it—even more aggressive postures on behalf of songwriters, publishers, and music creators. But things are significantly better than they were prior to the MMA.

Songs are a unique type of property. A song is not something you can sit on. It's not a chair. You can't drive it. You can't build a house on it. You can't pick it up and put it in your pocket and walk out a door with it. But it's no different to take someone's song for free than it is to walk into the shop of a master carpenter, pick out your favorite table, load it into your truck, and drive home with it. The carpenter's talent, time, and energy went into making that table. It would be called theft. And yet, when it comes to intellectual property, songs included, it's almost an invisible thing.

People hear it in their car. They hear it in their house. They just think it exists—like the wind or anything else—as if it were a natural fact that music is all around us and everybody has access to it. Well, everybody does have access to it. But those who created the music didn't just wake up one day with the skill set to make something that impacted, entertained, or inspired you. You got something out of it. There's a reason why people love music. They love it because of what it does for them—*because it helps them.*

Music changes their mood. It allows them to feel like they're not alone. Sometimes they hear a song or a songwriter say something. They're able to identify with it and say to themselves: "Wow, I'm not the only one who feels like that." Songwriters are able to attract millions and millions of people together around the same thought. It's a very powerful process—almost like magic because you can turn a blank sheet of paper into anything. More likely than not, whatever you put down on that paper will mean nothing. But every now and then, you might produce something valuable that has a dramatic impact on a lot of people.

I still think streaming grotesquely underpays people. And now that the whole world is streaming music, new songwriters can no longer get a decent publishing deal. It used to be that some new guy from Nebraska could move to Nashville, approach a publisher with 15 or 20 good songs, and get $30,000 for a publishing deal, which was adequate enough money. But those deals aren't there anymore. You're lucky to make half that these days, and after taxes, there isn't much left. Also, songwriters have day jobs to make ends meet, which means they're not able to devote their time fully to writing songs.

I've seen a lot of writers move back to the state they came from. *There's no telling how many writers we've missed* that might have taken songwriting to the next level simply because they couldn't afford to do it. So, why can't companies afford to give them a better deal? Their income has been decimated by streaming services. While songwriters will get paid more under the MMA, it's still a fraction of what it should actually be. The fact that the MMA was a unanimous, bipartisan decision signed by the President proves it was long overdue. I think there's more work to do, but the MMA is one hell of a platform to build upon.

If there's anything I would say to any consumer of music, it's this: Remember the analogy of the master carpenter. You don't just walk in and take his table. A songwriter is just as much of a craftsman. You don't just walk in and take their song for nothing, even if you can. Over time, I hope that our culture will come to see a song as real property. Somebody spent many years getting good enough to create what I just listened to, so I need to pay for that. It's all about integrity. We pay for things we like all the time, so what's the big deal about paying a dollar to add to your playlist? I think it's starting to break through to people. And if they do that, there will be a stronger foundation for more great music to come.

99

In the Act

THE MUSIC MODERNIZATION ACT is composed of three separate titles, as follows:

Title I: Musical Works Modernization Act

The Musical Works Modernization Act—formerly known as the Songwriter Equity Act—addressed the licensing of musical works. Perhaps the centerpiece of the MMA was the creation of a new entity to issue blanket licenses for streaming digital music. After an application and selection process in 2019, The Mechanical Licensing Collective was designated by the U.S. Copyright Office to become the new entity.

Digital service providers (DSPs) wanted the efficiency of a blanket license for mechanical royalties to end further liability entanglements with copyright infringement lawsuits. Songwriters and music publishers agreed to create, govern, and oversee The MLC in exchange for DSP support of changes in how songwriter royalty rates are set.

The MLC is responsible for gathering reports given by digital music providers, which it then uses to properly match each musical work to its owner(s) and distribute royalties accordingly. As of this writing, The MLC is working on an open database to make all of this information available to the general public. This database will identify and locate the copyright owners of any recording in their purview. If it so happens that The MLC is unable to match any musical works to their copyright owners, it will default to those owners listed in its records and distribute royalties based on the relative market shares found in existing usage reports of digital music providers.

In August 2017, the NSAI, the NMPA, and other groups were meeting in Washington, D.C., when the Digital Media Association (DiMA) proposed the blanket digital mechanical license. It was then that NSAI Executive Director Bart Herbison thought they might finally pass a music licensing bill after all those years.

The streaming services agreed to the outline of the Music Modernization Act, knowing that they would have to pay songwriters more. How are the streaming services able to do that? Streaming companies were fledgling services ten to twelve years ago and not bringing in that much capital. It's much different today, as they are taking in billions of dollars of revenue each year and can pay the songwriters more without paying record labels less. Each service was also paying millions to license these mechanical rights.

What was an individual cost for each company should now be reduced, as they can each take a percentage of those costs and collectively fund the new Mechanical Licensing Collective. **"**

There is also the Digital Licensee Coordinator (DLC) that organizes the actions of relevant licensees and assigns a non-voting representative to The MLC board. The MLC will face operational costs throughout this identification process, and these costs will be paid by digital music providers and voluntary contributors. The Copyright Royalty Judges will set an administrative assessment, subsequently applied as a nationwide standard. The MLC and the DLC will participate in proceedings to establish the administrative assessment before the Copyright Royalty Judges.

There will be no change to the current system that allows filing notices of intention (NOIs) when it comes to obtaining compulsory licenses for the manufacture and distribution of phonorecords of nondramatic musical works (although licensees may still serve NOIs directly on copyright owners). This will remain within the confines of the Copyright Office on a song-by-song basis, which will continue operation for non-digital uses, such as CDs and vinyl. The Copyright Office will *no longer accept* bulk NOIs with regard to digital records (i.e., downloads or interactive streams) of musical works.

License availability is restricted to royalties under the Interim Period license until January 2021, by which time the digital music provider must make reasonable efforts, in good faith, to match every song on its streaming service with the appropriate copyright owner. As the Copyright Royalty Judges set and apply new rates, these will be determined based on a "willing buyer/seller" standard, thereby replacing the standard under policy 801(b)(1). According to the new law:

The section 114(i) provision that prohibits performing rights organization (PRO) rate courts from considering licensing fees paid for digital performances of sound recordings in its rate-setting proceedings for the public performance of musical works is partially repealed. This repeal does not apply to radio broadcasters, as the MMA does not include a performance royalty for AM/FM airplay. Additionally, the legislation changes how judges in the Southern District of New York are assigned to the rate court proceedings set forth in the consent decrees for ASCAP and BMI, by assigning each new rate dispute on a rotating basis instead of all disputes being handled by the same judge.

Here, Bart Herbsion expounds upon the importance of the passage of the MMA.

There was no federal copyright protection for the sound recording copyright (meaning the record, which is called the musical work). Now there is, so if you wrote a song or recorded a song before 1972, because of the MMA, you're now guaranteed to be paid. The MMA accomplishes three very important goals. First, it extends certain federal copyright protections to sound recordings made prior to 1972. Second, it updates the way digital music providers obtain mechanical licenses and the way songwriters are compensated for digital mechanical royalties and for performance royalties. Third, it codifies a process for record producers and engineers to receive a portion of royalties for the sound recordings they helped to create. **"**

Copyright infringement attorneys were not enamored with the passage of the MMA. This is mainly because songwriters can no longer sue the respective streaming service companies for licensing their work incorrectly if the services use The MLC and follow guidelines found in the Music Modernization Act. Most recently, Eminem's publisher, Eight Mile Style sued Spotify for allegedly not licensing Eminem's 243 songs in the proper manner. Yet the MMA mitigates such actions by imposing a cutoff date of December 31, 2017. Eight Mile Style deemed this an unconstitutional move claiming that it violates due process and property rights. The lawsuit is still in progress as of this writing.

Title II: Classics Protection and Access Act

The Classics Protection and Access Act—formerly known as the Compensating Legacy Artists for their Songs, Service, and Important Contributions to Society (CLASSICS) Act—folds pre-1972 sound recordings into the batter of the federal copyright system and allows remedies for copyright infringement. The revamped Classics Act differentiates between the copyright for a sound recording and the copyright for a musical work. As previously stated, there are two copyrights embedded within the recording of a song: a copyright for the composition (i.e., the melody and lyrics), referred to as the "musical work," and a copyright for the actual sound recording.

Remedies for unauthorized use of these recordings are available for 95 years after the initial publication date, subject to additional periods that include:

1. Recordings before 1923—where the period ends on December 31, 2021.

2. Recordings from 1923-1946—where the period ends five years after the 95-year term.

3. Recordings from 1947-1956—where the period ends 15 years after the 95-year term.

4. And recordings from 1957-1972—where the period ends on February 15, 2067.

The Classics Act allows for statutory licensing of all non-interactive pre-1972 recordings that already apply to post-1972 recordings. In order for recording owners to be able to recover damages for the unauthorized use of their pre-1972 recordings, owners must file their recordings with the U.S. Copyright Office to become public records in place of the typical formal registration. Remedies are available for the unauthorized use of a sound recording 90 days after it has been indexed within the Office. Passage of the MMA allows entities to play pre-1972 recordings without facing legal consequences. To qualify for this exception, one must first file a "notice of noncommercial use." As long as the rights owner raises no objections to such use within 90 days of filing, rights to those recordings are granted with the expectation that they will be used in good faith.

Title III: Allocation for Music Producers (AMP) Act

Before the passage of the MMA, music producers, mixers, and/or sound engineers were not able to recover royalties from the streaming of sound recordings they helped create. Now, recording artists who agree to allocate a percentage of their royalties to a producer, mixer, or sound engineer can send a "letter of direction" (LOD) to SoundExchange.

In the case of sound recordings produced before November 1, 1995, SoundExchange defaults to a 2% royalty in the absence of a LOD. Moreover, the sound engineer, mixer, or producer under this exemption must adhere to the following requirements:

1. For a period of at least four months, the producer has made reasonable attempts to contact and request a letter of direction instructing SoundExchange to pay the producer, mixer, and/or sound engineer a portion of the royalties payable to the featured recording artist(s) without affirmation or denial.

2. After the receipt of certification and for a period of at least four months before SoundExchange's first distribution to the producer, mixer, and/or sound engineer, SoundExchange has attempted to contact the recording artists in a reasonable manner to notify them of the request.

3. And, SoundExchange has not received a written objection by the recording artist within ten business days before the first distribution of royalties goes to the producer, mixer, or sound engineer.

Due to the countless hours of hard work by many, the MMA has set a new standard for the future of music licensing, copyright, and distribution. The MMA is a unique instance in which both parties in Congress put politics aside to provide unanimous bipartisan support in both chambers—a feat hard to grasp in today's world. In the 21st century, there will be a staggering growth of intellectual property court cases due to the sheer amount of progress in technology. The passage of the MMA will mitigate some of this fallout, allowing songwriters to focus on what they do best: writing good songs that span generations and bring people together in a harmonious way.

When The Mechanical Licensing Collective fully begins operations in Nashville, it will collect royalties to pay songwriters, lyricists, composers, and music publishers. By creating a new legal, free-market standard that allows judges to set mechanical and performance royalty rates, songwriters should now receive higher pay. The MMA is, therefore, a beacon of hope that songwriters will finally be fairly compensated, leading to a stronger economy and a stronger United States of America.

SUMMARY OF SONGWRITER "GAINS" UNDER THE MUSIC MODERNIZATION ACT:

- Changed how songwriter mechanical royalties are set by replacing an outdated 1909 law that governed those royalties.
- Replaced the 1941 Department of Justice consent decree standards governing ASCAP and BMI performance royalties.
- The rules determining songwriters' payouts are now based on a "rate standard" comprised of a "willing buyer, willing seller" fair market value.
- Required the random selection of judges when performing rights societies, ASCAP or BMI, go to a rate court proceeding. Those judges were previously appointed for life.
- Instituted The MLC, governed by songwriters and music publishers, to oversee and administer digital mechanical licensing and payments,

resolve disputes, and administer unclaimed royalties.

- Streaming companies will pay for all of The MLC's costs, meaning for the first time in global history, songwriters will receive 100 cents on their digital mechanical royalty since streaming services foot the bill.

- Songwriters and music publishers will govern and operate The MLC—gaining unprecedented control over their own administration, collection, and payment processes.

- There will be a new, more fair, and efficient process for distributing unclaimed funds. The songwriters' share of this money will be based on their streaming activity for the distribution period, and songwriters without publishing deals will also be eligible to receive unclaimed funds through The MLC.

- For the first time in history, U.S. digital mechanical song ownership information will be contained in one completely transparent database administered by The MLC.

THE MUSIC MODERNIZATION ACT ALSO:

- Guaranteed royalty payments from streaming services to artists whose recordings were done before 1972. Those recordings did not previously have Federal copyright protection.

- Stipulated direct royalty payments from streaming companies to record producers and engineers.

THE WORD "RECORD" comes from the Old French *record*, meaning "memory, statement, or report." And so, the very concept of a record was always encoded with notions of authorship and accountability long before it came to mean "disk on which sounds or images have been recorded" in 1878. But what happens when records, as we once knew them, become a vestige of the past?

Despite a trending resurgence of interest in vinyl, the future of music looks to be resolutely digital. This means that the very concept of a record, in both the musical and legal sense, will change with the times. As music becomes more ephemeral in production and means of distribution, and in light of an industry need for the MMA's passage into law, we must think about what it means to attribute rights of ownership to that which might have no physical form.

With the rise and development of artificially intelligent technologies, some would say that music itself is in danger of becoming mechanized to the point where humans might no longer be at the center of its creation. Given that computer programs can spit out symphonies in a matter of minutes, and in the style of any composer who spent many years of their lives laboring over score sheets with quill in hand, who will we consider the rightsholders of such music to be? And will people be held legally accountable for (mis)using AI-composed music? It may be decades before such issues come to the attention of lawmakers as being worthy of serious concern, but the fact that the possibility exists should be enough to make us question the meaning of music to begin with.

All the more reason to hold on to music as a testament to the power of the human spirit—*a means of articulating what binds us* in this time of toxic political partisanship and social unrest—and to fairly recognize the efforts of those who offer it for all to share.

It has been an absolute delight working on this book and doing what I love by diving deep into the progression of technology, music, and law while touching on our current times and injustices imposed by our government. I've essentially lived on $3 a day for the past four months to self-fund *MODERNIZATION OF MUSIC* completely, and I'm grateful that you have lent your time to check out this art project of mine. The contents of this book have come from the bottom of my heart, and I hope you have enjoyed learning about the MMA.

Future rate court proceedings under the new rules of the Music Modernization Act should produce higher rates for songwriters. Living as we do in times increasingly divided along partisan lines, the rarity of such unanimous support around a single issue cannot be overstated. This is a rallying cry not only for the music industry but also for us as a nation to come together around something we all can agree on.

Like all professions, where there is top money, the top talent follows. With the advent of the MMA, the future for songwriting is bright. As our pop music is a direct reflection of where we stand in time, it is extremely important for the art to thrive in the hands of those who shape *the very sound of our age.* Songwriting is, therefore, more necessary than ever.

In these times of social distancing during COVID-19, we owe it to ourselves to use music as a force of harmony rather than division. Once the Music Modernization Act goes fully into effect on January 1, 2021, the world will sound better to all ears.

BIBLIOGRAPHY

- "Orrin G. Hatch-Bob Goodlatte Music Modernization Act," 115 P.L. 264

- "Classics Protection and Access Act." Copyright. gov. https://www.copyright.gov/music-modernization/pre1972-soundrecordings/

- "Musical Works Modernization Act." Copyright. gov. https://www.copyright.gov/music-modernization/115/

- "Allocation for Music Producers Act." Copyright.gov. https://www.copyright.gov/music-modernization/amp/

- Eight Mile Style, LLC v. Spotify United States Inc., 2020 U.S. Dist. LEXIS 58134

E. Maxwell & Manning

Made in the USA
Monee, IL
19 December 2020